MW01170134

Eye to Eye

The
Language of Energy
and
Horse

by Karen E. Nowak

Copyright © 2002 by Karen Elise Nowak

ISBN 0-7414-1274-8

Published by:

PUBLISHING.COM

519 West Lancaster Avenue
Haverford, PA 19041-1413
Info@buybooksontheweb.com
www.buybooksontheweb.com
Toll-free (877) BUY BOOK
Local Phone (610) 520-2500
Fax (610) 519-0261

Printed in the United States of America

Printed on Recycled Paper

Published October, 2002

Contents

Thank you to Helen Downs of Schuyler Editing for your expertise in polishing this book to the finished product.
&
Thank you to Joan Muller for adding the energy of your talents to grace the cover as well as the inside pages.

Introduction

1.

Advice is often a detriment to true progress. Only in individual stillness as prelude to, as emergent from, immersive spirit labor will come passage.

If there is a sense of self-annihilating that must be demanded in such a definition, so be it. Too much of our society already has lost daily personal responsibility and spiritual centeredness to indulgence. The dull indignity of indulgence is its life-line not to ethic, but to social practice and gratification.

2.

Abundance by annihilating, by becoming vessel.

Each true spiritual elder has engaged entrance in passage by vacancy and acute limit. This sort of affirmative indwelling requires an interdependent spirit in MOMENTUM as companion-stillpoint between both emergence and annihilation. Alignment to one side or the other, and opposing open fields break the momentum. Remember, what is always at stake is origin. Towards origin, there remains only vessel.

Karen Nowak's journey is an intensely confluent life centered as rhythmic mergeance to sacred principle. She sees all alive as a centerpiece-gift given purifying winds, and that centerpiece: placed at the very polarities of emergence and annihilation. If there is an eruptive landscape in Nowak's work, it is an effacing open-land where spirit sources into the surrounding space as resonance.

Karen's written work, Eye to Eye: the Language of Energy, and Horse carries an intensely personal space outward, as visual field, as vibrational threshold. Her work involves being immersed in the language of energy and reconnecting to the harmonic play between man and animal in union. The individual depth between two in union exists in both solace and shared being, an "island in dance."

3.

In aurealis, there is companion common space of light, and dark in reference.

Polarities rock each other, always, to erasure. Released, rather than structured by such constant connection, Eye to Eye documents an homage to both the dark, as visitation--and light, as healing convergence of horse and human woven in articulate bond.

Encounter as medicine to intensely inner life, bound.

If there were no other apparent event of passage, horse and human in mutual awareness would woven in spirit grieve difference. What makes a book such as Eye to Eye effortlessly sever what we know from what we would know, is that difference is empty to difference, and wholly and abundant center-still to common life.

Timothy A Shea
July 2002

For all the animal and human spirits I have been blessed to have as part of my world.

The Language of Energy

We are simultaneously
blessed and cursed
by
our left brain
analytical
thinking.

In sharing the information contained in the following
pages, my
intention is to offer guidelines for which you will
resonantly
experience energy,
satisfy the need to understand and spiritually make
sense of
your right brain intuitive side,
and also
exercise your ability to
trust your own senses.

We are all here for
our own
earthly experience.
We speak
the same verbal language,
yet we interpret
information differently.

May we together
find common ground
to travel
the language
of energy!

Has anyone ever seen
the
emotional
vibration
of
Love?

We have been recipients
of it,
have given it,
been touched by it,
seen the results of it,
yet we can't physically touch it,
and
we still
believe
it exists.

It was not so many years ago
that electricity was foreign,
yet today we easily forget about,
yet rely on,
something
we
can't
see.

Kirilian photography has shown
that we all have an energy field,
referred to as
the auric body,
which extends beyond
the physical.

Viewing ourselves as mental, emotional, and
spiritual beings encased in physical bodies
we change our focus
from
strictly the physical
to
the multidimensional
and
consequently shift
our perspective.

If we think of the auric body as a muscle
we are learning to strengthen,
just as a new born child learns to
strengthen its physical body, we can begin
to comprehend the path of learning
a new language.

Learning to recognize and work with
energy
is not
a quick fix-
but
a journey,
not
some great mystery-
but simply working with
universal
laws.......

You will only get out of this work
what
you are willing
to
put
in

and,

you will only be able to understand
in an animal
what
you are willing to travel to
in
yourself.

There in
Lies
the
D
E
P
T
H
of
our

COMMITMENT

When man first attempted
verbal communication through
the vibration of the vocal-chords,
what later became known as
speech was born.

In early man,
survival necessitated
the use of all one's senses
in conveying
and receiving information.

Man, during his evolution, narrowed
and came to believe
that the verbal was the critical
and only means
of communication.
As a large portion of the civilization
became less in touch
with the responsibility
of personally
fulfilling their immediate needs
in the move from predominately rural,
to city and suburban life,
survival took on a different meaning,
and our desire to stay open
on all auric levels
was replaced
by a need for protection
of a different kind.

Our sensory perceptions
were assaulted,
and personal space allotment
became challenged.
The verbal
became the dominant
and sometimes only
means of communication.

Animals, in contrast,
never veered from being
complete auric sensors
for vibrational information.
They remain
open receptors
for hearing the voices that speak
throughout
the body.

We are all vibrational
auric beings,
with
physical,
emotional,
mental,
and
spiritual
aspects.

We limit the ways in which
we may
access
information
when we remain
in
the belief system
of
the
spoken word
as
the only
vibration
that
speaks.

At one time or another we have all experienced
discomfort associated with someone,
or someplace,
that feeling
was energy.

When we know
something is wrong with our horse,
or any of our animals,
without any outward signs from them,
that is energy; we are listening
to
our intuitive self
pick up on
the
imbalance
in another
spiritual being.

We have not completely
lost
the ability
to hear
what is
being
communicated,
it
has just become

dormant.

As speech was once very primitive
and took time to become
as sophisticated as
it is today,
so too
is
the re-evolution
of our use
and
understanding
of vibrational energy
with its
subtle
and
intricate
inner frequencies.

The Universe has provided us with
its
laws.

Whether we choose
to
use them is
up
to
us.

Everything on earth is a vibration resonating at a different rate, therefore the entire auric body of humans and animals is a vibration speaking it's own language. Energy vibrations manifest at different densities, the physical being the densest vibration manifesting as the human body and all we can **see** around us. The mental vibration manifests as our thoughts, the emotional as things we feel such as joy or sorrow, and the spiritual as our relationship to a power greater than we are.

Following these thoughts the physical vibration resonating against a mental, emotional or spiritual vibration speaks out in a multitude of voices. Working with energy we are able to segregate, identify and hold open a space surrounding a specific voice and introduce universal healing energy allowing the new vibration to accelerate change to a peaceful state.

In working with any species we are given the privilege of learning, it is a gift that is ours to be cherished if we so choose.

My inner dialogue follows a journey and learning to trust that journey has not come over night. I had preconceived notions as to how this would all come out on paper but the universe had other ideas.

When awakening to the language of energy with the
animal kingdom,
one of the first shifts in perspective
comes
in recognizing the confluence of :
animal,
you, and
the energy created between the two.
One affects the other,
constantly changing
what is
created
in
confluence.
This, on the surface,
may seem a very simple statement,
but how many times
do we come to our horses,
or any of our animals, with
the thought that
a behavior they are presenting
is not somehow connected to us,
or vice versa?
We are not always responsible for,
but we are always affected by,
the vibrational energy
being emitted.

Just as the effect
of a pebble thrown into a pond
ripples out,
so too do vibrations of energy.

We may come to our quadrupeds
with a little too much
forward in our minds
and
energy fields,
and they may react to this,
or they may have something going on
(for we are not the only ones
who can have an off day),
and we
come transilient and ready to ride,
ignoring
the messages they are giving.
Not staying focused
and conscious
of what is being created
between us,
there-by
not staying aware
of what we are contributing
integrally,
and
in orchestration,
is often at the center
of some disappointment,
or even
what appears on the surface
as
failure.
For many of us, the energy
retained in our energetic data bases,
known as
FAILURE
stems from
two energy beings:

you and your horse,
understanding
the same thing
differently,
and
not yet finding the key
to the other's understanding.
Expectations
of
right/wrong
black/white
creates a patterned response.
In working with the energy of what you are reading and
how it is   laid   on the page,
we too are creating
a mutual understanding of
the language of energy.
Staying conscious,
present, and non-judgmental
when we are with
our horses
begins
the process
of building our energetic muscles,
and our ability
to sense them on all
levels.
We are energetically connected to the animals in our
lives at all times, and
when something
is amiss with our horse,
or any of our companions
in the animal kingdom,
it affects
confluence.

Horses function by reading energy,
and they read yours.
Animals communicate,
each using its own set of body language and energy of
intent,
perceiving energy vibrations
as a way of being.
Their spoken language utilizes intricate vibration
patterns,
which as we re-connect
to our innate abilities
will reveal itself.
In the shift away from being responsible for our every
need at the most
basic level -
our listening skills
lost their energetic muscle tone.

Being aware of the smallest whisper
of our environment
to communicate information
is a part of our energetic,
and cellular base.
We have stored the belief
in our chakra system
that
we are not responsible for
and need not be in sinc with
our environment,
and
therefore, do not resonate
its unfiltered dialogue.

This belief system when brought to light
is not in fitting
with
universal law.

In listening
with **all** of our being
to the earth and its creatures,
we begin
to
reconnect.

Horses are entities
of great lineage.
They are not gym equipment.

Every day people ask animals to behave in a human
manner to make it easier for us to coexist, and being
the honorable beings that they are, they try and often
times succeed.

But how often do we honor their essence?

It is not always possible to allow them to live as their
ancestors did, but despite the domestication process,
they still retain the purity of who they are. Honoring
their spirit you are there - by connecting in a non verbal
manner and offering another level of communion.

This information helps in transmuting our old belief
systems of separateness
to a knowing
connectedness.
Animals are multidimensional beings just as we are,
and
opening to ways of being that will enhance
communication strengthens the relationship
and brings it to another
level.
Treated with dignity
and respect,
as the partners
that they are,
our horses
will truly dance with us
in this journey
we are
both on.
There are no coincidences,
and your horse is in your life for lessons
and vice versa for him/her. No one is less or greater
than the other, for we are all spiritual beings.
When we learn to hear with more than just our physical
ears, we take yet another step into their world of
understanding.
This applies to all species.

Animals come to us with purity of intention and
respond favorably when treated in like manner.
Working with them involves commitment,
for to communicate on non verbal levels and
consciously work with the unseen takes clearing of old
patterns
and requires you to think outside the box which you
have become accustomed to function comfortably.
When we stretch our own or our animal's comfort zone
in a conscious open manner we open the space for
growth to occur. Animals are spiritual beings of great
magnitude and wisdom, and every spiritual being is
equal in the eyes of the universal greatness.
When we choose to live in harmony with universal
laws, an awaiting world unfolds.

We
need
only
follow
the
t
h
r
e
a
d

**Intention
Puts
Energy in Motion!**

Your **intention** and active presence in reading what is presented in these pages will affect the journey.

INTENTION
PUTS ENERGY IN MOTION

A very simple yet powerful gift that universal law has given us:

"What goes around comes around" "Watch what you ask for you may get it" "Your words create" are all statements that wield more energy than we had previously been aware. Intentions sent out need fertile soil to return to. If we place barriers up, respond with old stored energy, or do not prepare a place for the energy return, the energy vibrates off the last message it receives, and if our belief system is narrow, it will return to us as we expect to hear it. If we go out on a ride and ask (our intention) that our horse pass through a place where he always spooks, hoping, yet not fully believing, that this time will be different. We get there, and he/she spooks. We have a responsibility in the equation. We had not healed our original belief system, therefore, the spooking is what was created. We had not stayed open, envisioning what it was we <u>did</u> want.

When there is lack of clarity it leaves an escape,
for there is comfort in not risking,
not creating what we really do want, not only with our
horses, but in all aspects of our lives.
This is a very simple example, but the universal law
stands true no matter where applied.
I was riding with a friend who told me the horse I was
on spooked at a certain place on the trail. We agreed
she shouldn't tell me where until after we had passed
through. The horse never spooked. I agree, it is a
great deal harder when you already have the
information of where the fear would come in, but
changing energy takes practice and commitment.

As self trust is built
and
we stay open
to new experiences and thought patterns,
we begin exploring what it means for energy to return
for our highest healing good, bringing us the lessons
which will enhance our personal growth.

When we are working with our horse, and we send out
an **intention** to create a certain response
and then do not receive it the path our intention energy
takes to return what was asked
or even
something better,
takes the path
of traveling through our horse's physical, mental,
emotional, and spiritual body -
filtering through his/her level of understanding -
returning to us
as their best effort to respond.
As a higher lesson, the intention sent out came back as
greater understanding.

Following the path of the intention sent out shows us
where communication and understanding ended,
where we were not clear in what we asked or knew to
ask. Preparing a space for greater understanding, in
even the simplest situation, enhances and deepens
your relationship with your horse.
Using an open energy field, we receive information of
any miscommunication. Staying open to the intricacies
of how the law works can be an amazing experience
when viewed from a place of
non-judgment,
bringing knowledge we might otherwise have missed.
Perhaps we are able to view how our horse learns, how
we
communicate information, or even how we view our
relationship:
is it a two way communication
or a one way, and are we willing
to look
at what our horses are reflecting back to us.

I could go on but only you, with an open heart and mind, will know which road to walk. Through this process, flexing our energy muscles blesses us with a closer relationship to these miraculously spiritual beings.

At the onset this may appear as too much work, but built upon slowly, as you look back, it will reveal a journey only you and your wonderful equine friend could take.
As a child,
when you first realized you had hands,
you didn't know what you could do with them,
and they where pretty uncontrollable and foreign,
but as you grew,
they evolved into
tools we take for granted-
yet look at what they do.

Vibrations,
including intentions
affect
every aspect of our lives,
and
the same stands true for our horses or any animal we
interact with.
When we still ourselves
through
whatever means we choose,
whether it be
Reiki, meditation, yoga,
or any other stilling practice,
we begin
to consciously travel
our
own inner road.
We are only as good a channel
as we are able
to go to
within
ourselves.

Living
using only our left brain analytical thinking
keeps us on the surface, a one dimensional plane.
If we choose to change, we need to step out of our
previous thought patterns
and
explore other possibilities.

Keeping a space open to consciously
interact with
and be part of
the energy change
brings us to yet
another level of union.
If you are not accustomed to viewing yourself
as a multidimensional being,
it is difficult
to see our animals in that light.
When I became consciously aware of the journey I was on,
I was still at that point unaware of the depths to which I
would have to go within myself. Learning inner trust takes
time and patience, and grows with each step and with the
commitment you are willing to make at each turn. We are
learning to live in a manner whereby our road map is
drawn from information found within ourselves.

The
Healing Session

An animal comes to a healing session with a purity
to which we can aspire.
The definition of a healing session can encompass
many things when we broaden the scope of our belief.
Healing comes on many levels and occurs in more than
just the physical level. Sometimes a healing needs to
be on mental emotional levels. Healing can even mean
leaving the body and crossing over, otherwise known
as death.
When we travel our inner road we open to the honesty
our equine companions are offering us.

I wish I could say "do this to get this result" but the
equation is <u>always</u> different. There are **guidelines**
offered, but the teachers are many, and each presents
a unique lesson to explore possibilities and work with
what information resonates true for you.

In working with any spiritual being,
follow
the lesson laid before you.
When we are not accustomed
to trusting ourselves and our instincts,
we look for a place to start.

Reading others' journeys and perceptions,
and/or
working with others you feel comfortable with
takes courage. To do something different
adds to the data you can draw from
if the information rings true to you,
ultimately culminating
in
Trusting
YOUR SELF
and your perceptions.
Learning to recognize and isolate different energies
goes hand in hand with
trusting
yourself
and what you perceive.
Learning that the Universe will provide
the information needed
for everyone's highest healing good,
brings one to a place of trust.
There are benefits to set patterns of thinking,
such as not risking change
and possibly
finding ourselves in uncharted waters.
Our defenses have kept us safe,
just as they do in our horses and in all animals,
and they will continue to do what they have to do
until we recognize them, thank them for what they are
doing,
and commit and make it our intention
to
take
the next step.
The defensive energies will transmute
and
heal in our animals as well as in ourselves.

Depending on your own
and your animal's journeys,
many levels of exploration will take place,
defenses being only one.
Living consciously
opens up a whole new world .
This process is a journey
and
you are right where you are meant to be,
for it is all part of the lesson.
It is no coincidence you are reading this
at this moment,
for there is
a
thread
that will take you to your next step,
even if
the page looks

empty.

Animals read you before you enter their energy zone. When coming to a session, it is helpful to energetically cleanse, to take a moment to let go of and release anything that is not beneficial to the session, optimizing communication. Stripping away unnecessary vibrations, we start with a cleaner slate so the animal is not concerned about something we might bring, therefore maintaining a focused work space. This can be as simple as taking deep breadths and releasing tension.

Start examining what you are sensing from the animal as you approach and honor what your intuition is telling you. All beings, including animals, have an energy field that surrounds them called an aura. Be aware when you are about to enter theirs, and mentally ask permission and honor what you sense. Should the animal tell you not to come in yet, listen to that message.

The animal must know first that he/she can trust you.

A horse by the name of Victor, I recently had the pleasure to meet, graciously agreed to partner with me at a demonstration at a local university. When it came time to start, and we were in front of the audience, Victor said "I can't let you in" and proceeded to move around not letting me touch him. It took a moment to explain to the audience what was going on. Since Victor had various students on his back and in his energy field on a regular basis in an attempt to protect himself, he went inside and internalized his emotional pain (a healthy energy field surrounds the body) therefore, he absorbed something from each of the humans, who well meaning or otherwise left energetic residue on his spiritual being. He was bracing to carry and not release it all, thus the sore back.

I am sure there were some in the audience who just scoffed, dismissed, and did not understand. (Have you ever been around a person who made you feel really uncomfortable even after they had left? They had left an energetic residue.) The physical reasons for Victor's back issues being a lot of new riders, but energetically, he was retaining energy in a way he could handle to protect himself from the emotional pain of not being respected as more than gym equipment. Because he was a school horse he was not able to attach to anyone. If he did, when the student left, he was left hurting, and he just couldn't go there. Too many separations for his heart. When I told Victor energetically that I honored what he was telling me and would not force my energy on him he quieted.

THE FIRST PRIORITY
IS
ALWAYS THE ANIMAL

I had to risk what the audience thought to honor Victor.
That is not noble, it is simply universal law. If we want
to be honored in the same way in our lives, we must
work with what is presented,
then
honor,
trust,
and
let go.
The foundation of any session must be built on trust.
Focus on what you feel when entering the animals
presence. What was your first sensation? Did you
sense fear, apprehension,
pain, nothing, or something you couldn't identify?
When we are working with our own animal, each
session and each step can reflect not only their issues,
but ours as well. If that strikes a chord of uneasiness,
joy, or confusion, good because it is a place to start.
You will be traveling places that will encompass a
multitude of emotions. Take each experience and be
present with it as long as you can, and
<u>do not judge</u>
how long you were able to focus or, the subject matter.
No Judgment! It is not uncommon to be very critical
of ourselves. Accepting who we are without judgment
begins the healing process. It also helps us accept our
animals for who they are, thereby giving us a starting
point to move forward instead of going around the
gerbil wheel again and again, not getting anywhere but
right where we started.

48

When I jumped off the gerbil wheel, I was astounded at how many times I would put myself down in the course of a day, or for that matter in an hour, and how restrictive my thoughts and patterns where. I responded with old patterns that were no longer appropriate, such as getting frustrated with not understanding and putting myself down for being the **only** person who couldn't get it no matter what! It was a way I could protect myself from risking. It has taken time to be able to be present in situations, and each time, I am presented with new challenges to stay there. I am still learning there are plenty of times for me to stop being judgmental of not only myself but of others.

If it hasn't become apparent yet, there are many directions which things can take after the first step of asking permission to enter into an animals space in such a focused manner.
Assuming you have received permission proceed slowly and try to keep your mind clear. Again, you can see the analogy of learning a new language, because the more sessions you participate in, the clearer the voice of the vibration becomes, and it will become easier for you to interpret what you receive with more than your eyes and ears. We are all observant with more than the commonly used senses; we just need to strengthen the trust in the information we receive.

Ask the animal where he/she would like you to start. Some animals are more communicative than others and will tell you exactly what they want and position their bodies as such. Others will not be comfortable communicating in such a fashion with a human, but would still like you to work - start where you are intuitively guided, and if in doubt, start at the middle of the back. When starting in the middle of the back on a horse, you are positioning yourself in a safe zone if he/she should decide they don't want anything to do with this.

If you make it clear to the animal their comfort is your #1 priority,
and ask them to move away if they are uncomfortable, they will generally honor that.
When I receive permission I often start in the middle of the back. You can raise your hands slightly above the animals back and move slowly horizontally in either direction until you
feel a change in the sensation you are experiencing. Stop over that spot, and you can place your hands back on the body or remain slightly above, which ever is more comfortable for you both. Stay in that position for a few minutes while trying to sense what you are feeling. (At this point you are just beginning to trust your senses and identify what it is you see or sense, perceptions grow stronger with practice) If you sense it is time to move,
do it.
Scan the body again for the next chakra, which is where you feel the next sensation change. Be careful when you are at the root chakra, especially with a horse; it is where their fight or flight instinct originates, and if trust has not yet been established, they will not be comfortable with you there.
When first starting it may be simplest to start with looking for a physical trauma and simply
be an open channel for the animal to receive universal energy to heal. For we are all channels for healing energy. As you can see it can be as simple or as deep as you are willing to go in yourself, for again, you can not understand something in them that is more than the physical, if you haven't been to it in yourself.

Working with energy we are able to segregate, identify and hold open a space surrounding specific voices introducing universal healing energy and allowing the new vibration to accelerate change to a peaceful state. In working with any species we are given the privilege of learning, it is a gift that is ours to cherish if we so choose.

An
Energy Observation

The following guidelines are for strengthening your powers of observation. As you become more adept at remaining present and focused, and record information received through all of your senses, information will be revealed from the picture that extends beyond the situation.

Choose an animal you would like to work with and record in a journal your reasons for choosing that animal. If you don't have any definite feelings, record that; anything is okay. Write down any word that comes to mind, it need not be a full sentence. If you receive permission, record how you sensed it: "I just felt it," "I just knew," what you record need not be in depth. If you do not receive the okay, write that down and what feeling came up for you around this, then choose another animal.

When the animal has been chosen (in this case a horse), begin by becoming familiar with when you enter his/her personal space, the aura. Extend your arms out, away from your body at shoulder level, to enable you to feel any changes with the chakras in your hands. When first beginning, the energy vortices in your hands will be the easiest for you to sense energy. Your perceptions from other parts of your auric being will reawaken with the more energy work you do.

Stop when you sense a change, observe with your eyes what is happening with your horse. Is the horse uncomfortable, or is it accepting your presence, and on what level?

Speak to the horse, s/he may not understand the words, but will perceive on some level the intention that you present. Be honest; be open.

Trust is paramount in continuing to deeper levels of exploration.

At each step record, after your session is complete, any information that you can remember or that comes to you at the time. Recording your responses and feelings as well as what you sense the horse is feeling will begin to teach you the language of energy that is perceived with more than eyes and ears. Our, and our horse's reactions paint a much larger picture when recorded and connected over time.

The first day of your energy observation can be as simple as finding the space where you begin to perceive the aura. It can also be as complex as exploring the energy that is created between the union of both beings in an energy space. Commitment and intention will guide you.

Subsequent steps and days will be guided by your inner voice.

If you feel guided to begin touching your quadruped, an option is to work your way up or down the seven major chakras, again recording information from both parties. There are many scenarios that can occur, for each of our paths is different. The animal will guide you when given a space to work.

Working in this fashion for five sessions, whether they are subsequent or intermittent days is not important; but recording what is found is important.

Taking time to open and to be receptive takes inner exploration, which is a mighty teacher when given a chance.

Enjoy the teachers, for they are many, and work without judgment if possible.

When presented with an energy, if you choose, for it is always a choice, stay with it as long as possible, and speak with it. Energy will speak and reveal information that is beneficial to both entities involved. If you sense fear, ask to speak to it; it may reveal information beyond the surface level that pertains not only to your horse, but to yourself. Energy will speak to us - again it takes practice.

How deep you want to go is up to you
and
your equine companion.

**Introduction
To
The Chakra System**

When beginning to work with the chakra system you will be working with the mental, emotional, spiritual, and physical aspects of the body. Humans and animals are all multi-level beings with numerous energy vortices (chakras) vibrating throughout the physical self. An entire book could be written on just the chakra system, and many have been. What follows is a brief description of the chakra system and it is not meant to be a comprehensive statement, but simply an introductory guide.

There are seven major chakras, as illustrated in diagram one and two. The first chakra, known as the root, is located at the base of the spine and correlates to the adrenal glands. In the metaphysical, it is where we store our survival instinct, and in our horse, the flight or fight instinct. It is also where we are grounded and have our connection to the earth.

The second chakra is known as the sacral, and in the physical body, it affects the gonads. In the metaphysical it governs our awareness of others and how we interact with them.

The Third chakra is known as the solar plexus. In the physical it is near the pancreas. In the metaphysical, it is where emotions are rooted, where we get our gut feelings: it is our place of personal power and will.

The fourth chakra is the heart and correlates to the thymus gland, affecting the immune system in the physical body. In the spiritual body, it works with our ability to love. It is the point at which we balance our body and mind, and our upper and lower chakras.

The fifth chakra is the throat, and is associated with the thyroid gland in the physical. In the metaphysical, it takes the form of communication on all levels of the body. The sixth chakra is known as the third eye, and is near the pituitary gland. In the auric body, it is the place at which we have a heightened sense of awareness and at which we use the powers of the mind.

The final major chakra is the crown, and in the physical is located at the top of the head near the pineal gland. In the metaphysical, it is the point at which we connect to that which is beyond, to what is referred to as God, where all is connected.

Diagram
1

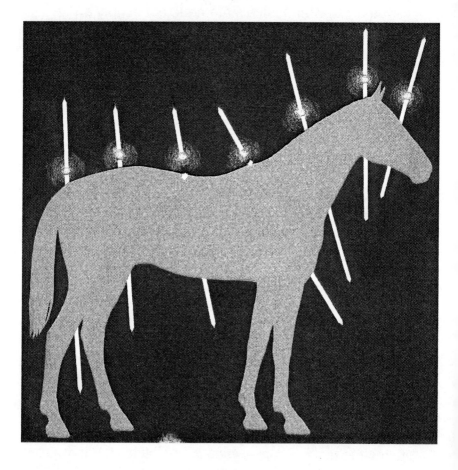

The illustrations of the horse and horse and rider are meant to be a guideline, a point from which to start your own discovery.

Diagram
2

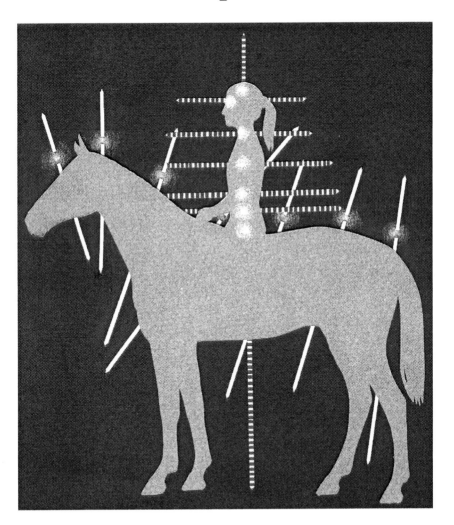

Common Space
An Equine Meditation

Common space is a mutual agreement to share the same energy

In the following meditation,
with your intention
as your guidance,
you will enter
common space.
The following may be adapted to any spiritual creature
we inhabit the earth with, if they consent. Always ask
permission, and proceed when you receive it.

This example will be done with an equine companion.

The meditation may be done while simply standing next
to your horse with your hands resting in a comfortable
position somewhere on his/her body, or while astride
with your root in the area of the solar plexus and heart
chakras.
Which ever you choose is up to you. If you are astride,
and the horse chooses to move, that is okay also, for
we work under mutual agreement with what is
presented
This meditation will be done astride.
Your main focus will be on your horse with the intention
that an equal energy will travel through you. It is not
necessary, but if you are able, focus on both your
horse and yourself. If you would like, the meditation
may be read to you by a friend.

Now that you have found the position, you are guided to:

1. Take 2 to 3 deep breaths, long slow inhales, envisioning healing white light, and as you release in a long slow exhale, envision releasing any energy you no longer need.

2. Put your attention on and project your perception to the bottom of your horses left hoof (and your left foot). Envision, or simply think of, the color red coming up from the earth into the left hoof. Take your time and give both you and your horse time to become aware of the energy. Follow the energy of the color red up the left leg to the left hip. Rest the fingers of your left hand gently on you horse's hip. Again, take your time, and let the energy rise at its own pace. When you sense it reaches your finger tips gently encourage it over the horses root chakra (in the area of the top of the tail). Envision the energy swirling in the vortex of the root, releasing/receiving what is beneficial to the ride. Your intention for the highest healing good will open the space for the work to occur. At the time you feel guided, gently switch hands in a fluid motion, and place your right fingers on the horses right hip, and encourage the energy down the right side through the hoof and into the earth (for this and all the remaining chakras allow the flow to occur simultaneously in your body).

3. Slowly begin to envision the color orange beginning to come up through the left hoof, again, while placing your hand on the left hip. Allow the slow progression of the energy as it follows the path of the physical body up the leg to the left hip. Sense as it passes by your finger tips and rises past the area of the root chakra to the sacral (in the area of the croup in your horse and around the navel area in yourself).

Sense the whirling of the vortex and the release. Gently switch hands to the right hip, and allow the energy to flow down the right leg at its own rate, back into the earth.

4. Call up from the earth the energy of the color yellow as you again rest you finger tips on the left hip. Sense it as it comes in through the left hoof, working its way up the leg to the area of the hip, and follow its progression through the body as it rises to the area of the solar plexus (approximately in the area beneath where you are sitting on your horse, or slightly behind, depending on the horse, and between the bottom of your lungs). Remain at the vortex, and experience what is being felt. Again, when you sense it is time, change hands and place your right hand on your horses right side, following the energy progression back down to the earth.

5. Following the same path, from the earth up through the left hoof and moving the finger placement to the left side of the heart chakra, begin the journey again, using the color green. When the energy rises to the heart, allow it to start flowing down the left leg, and experience the sensation of the vortex allowing the energy to flow down the right front leg, and proceeding with the return trip when ready, allowing the energy to flow down the rear leg and back to the earth.

6. Using the energy of the color blue, travel the same path up the body to the throat chakra, allowing the energy to simultaneously flow down the left front leg, placing the fingers of the left hand only as far up the horses body as is comfortable, without drastically changing your body position. When ready again, change hands and allow the energy to flow down the right front leg and back down the right side into the earth.

7. Next comes the color purple: follow the path past the previous chakras to the third eye (the space between and slightly above the physical eyes),and follow the guidelines of the previous chakras.

8. Using the energy of white light, follow the path up the left side, allowing the energy to again flow down the left leg. As your left hand rests gently on your horse, follow the energy up and out the crown chakra. Begin to feel the free flow as your horse connects energetically to the universe. Follow the energy back down the right front leg and then down the right side, and reconnect to the earth. Remain with the feeling for you are opening up to a dialogue of your own. The flow of energy from the earth to the heavens will open both you and your horse to a new level of communication.

The more times I have done this with my horse, the more we both have come to look forward to the union.

Follow your own inner voice, and find your common space, for these are only guidelines.

A Next Step

The interplay
between
man and horse
goes far deeper
than
the
physical (Equine)/physical (Human)
level.
In referring to the drawing of chakras for both man and
horse,
you are able to see
that for man, the energy vortexes run horizontally,
heading out into the ether of the earth,
running parallel to the earth and heavens.

In our equine companions the vortexes run vertically,
heading directly into the earth and heavens,
Is it any wonder they are grounded
and in touch with the heavens
in a way, we as upright Homo sapiens
cannot
completely
understand or remember?

When we have the privilege
to enter their energy field while being astride,
our vortexes intersect with theirs at a
90 degree angle.
Our 2nd through 6th chakras
run directly into
our horses
2nd (sacral) behind us,
and
into the 4th (heart) chakra in the front.
The interplay of energy in those areas
is very strong and direct.

When we are astride,
with our root directly on their solar plexus,
we are even closer;
we are totally immersed.

In most everyday living,
we are outside of one another's' energy fields,
respecting boundaries
and not entering in
unless
invited.
The majority of our encounters
are kept
"on the surface"
outside of our auras.
We spiritually,
and then mentally,
check others out
long before
we let them in
close.

We do not
act
in like fashion
with our horses.

We daily
enter in
and out
of their auras,
their energy space,
without
acknowledgment
of the spiritual etiquette
we give to most humans.

By studying
the messages that they send us,
we are privileged
to see into a world
we are only beginning
to know
exists.

Animals
are
our
teachers
in oh so many ways,
many of which are opening
to
YOU
now.

Contact Karen at:

Freedom Reins
Karen E. Nowak
90 Crystal Pond Rd.
Woodstock Valley, CT
06282

or:

freedomreins@earthlink.net